101 Successful Interviewing Strategies

ERIC KRAMER

Course Technology PTR

A part of Cengage Learning

COURSE TECHNOLOGY
CENGAGE Learning™

Australia, Brazil, Japan, Korea, Mexico, Singapore, Spain, United Kingdom, United States

COURSE TECHNOLOGY
CENGAGE Learning

101 Successful Interviewing Strategies
Eric Kramer

Publisher and General Manager, Course Technology PTR:
Stacy L. Hiquet

Associate Director of Marketing:
Sarah Panella

Manager of Editorial Services:
Heather Talbot

Marketing Manager:
Mark Hughes

Senior Acquisitions Editor:
Mitzi Koontz

Project and Copy Editor:
Kate Shoup

Interior Layout:
Shawn Morningstar

Cover Designer:
Mike Tanamachi

Proofreader:
Sandi Wilson

Printed in the United States of America
1 2 3 4 5 6 13 12 11

For product information and technology assistance, contact us at **Cengage Learning Customer and Sales Support, 1-800-354-9706.**

For permission to use material from this text or product, submit all requests online at **cengage.com/permissions.**

Further permissions questions can be e-mailed to **permissionrequest@cengage.com.**

Library of Congress Control Number: 2011920279

ISBN-13: 978-1-4354-5982-3

ISBN-10: 1-4354-5982-2

Course Technology, a part of Cengage Learning
20 Channel Center Street
Boston, MA 02210
USA

Cengage Learning is a leading provider of customized learning solutions with office locations around the globe, including Singapore, the United Kingdom, Australia, Mexico, Brazil, and Japan. Locate your local office at: **international.cengage.com/region.**

Cengage Learning products are represented in Canada by Nelson Education, Ltd.

For your lifelong learning solutions, visit **courseptr.com.**
Visit our corporate Web site at **cengage.com.**

This book is dedicated to Zachary and Jake, the future and hope of the American workforce and terrific sons.

I also dedicate this book to the thousands of job seekers whose wisdom, experience, and insights coalesced to guide the content of this book. Job searching and interviewing are two of life's most challenging and disheartening undertakings. All job seekers, as they persevere day-to-day searching for a job to provide for their families and themselves, are unrecognized heroes. I hope this book helps these heroes find jobs they love and earn the money they deserve.

Contents

Part 1

Interview Preparation:
Be Fully Prepared to Interview Well........................**1**

Part 2

Interview Attitude:
Being Prepared Mentally to Present Your Best......25

Part 3

Interview Tactics:
Making the Most of the Interview......................39

Table of Contents

Part 4

Managing the Interviewer:
Connect Through Curiosity and Conversation.......81

Part 5

The Interview Presentation:
Be More Persuasive with a Printed Presentation ...99

Part 6

After the Interview: It's Not Over Yet

About the Author

Eric Kramer is a "serial careerist," having held 10 jobs in six distinctly different careers. Eric knows interviewing!

Eric started his professional career as a clinical psychologist, has managerial experience in both large and small companies, has owned a software-development company, worked as an IT project manager, and sold large-scale mental-health–management software. Eric also worked as a career consultant and career-center manager with two of the country's largest job-transition firms. In these positions, Eric worked with hundreds of job seekers individually and in groups, helping them develop career visions, teaching them job-search skills, and coaching them through interviews.

In addition to this book, Eric has authored *101 Successful Networking Strategies*. He is identified as a recruiting thought leader by Kennedy Information, writes the *Interview Your Best* blog (http://employmentinterview.wordpress.com/), and tweets as Interview_Best. Eric also developed the iBest Interview Presentation, http://www.interviewbest.com, a presentation job candidates develop and bring to their interviews to communicate their fit with the job requirements, differentiate themselves, and win interviews. Eric is a frequent presenter at local and national conferences on the subjects of interview presentations, online identity optimization, and career management.

Eric earned a bachelor's degree in Psychology from the University of Hartford and a master's degree in Counseling Psychology from American University. He is certified in positive psychology coaching and is licensed as a psychologist in the state of Pennsylvania.

Introduction

Congratulations! You landed an interview, and now you have a great opportunity to get the job. Interviews are always a challenge; however, with good preparation, a set of positive thoughts, and a strategy to win, you will impress the interviewer, beat your competition, and succeed in the interview. Winning your interview will require powerfully communicating your qualifications for the job combined with the right interviewing behaviors. You're invited to the interview, so your qualifications and background are solid. Now all you have to do is start thinking the right way about your interview so you can communicate clearly and perform interview winning behaviors.

The right behaviors become far easier when you think the right thoughts. Correct thinking leads to correct doing. For example, to act confident, you have to think positive; to respond to tough interview questions correctly, you have to think about your goals when answering. This book will give you the right mental attitude by suggesting ways to think, followed by quick-to-learn, easy-to-implement strategies you can put into action to win the interview and land the job.

Good luck on your interview!

Eric Kramer, M.Ed.

1

Interview Preparation: Be Fully Prepared to Interview Well

1.

Know the Basics of Answering Any Question

What to Think

There are hundreds of possible interview questions. You cannot guess which ones will be asked, nor can you develop answers for all of them.

What to Do

Because you cannot prepare for all possible questions, focus on the basics of responding to any interview question. The most basic rules are as follows:

- Be positive.

- Focus on what you can contribute to the company.

- When possible, use examples of successes from previous jobs to demonstrate your abilities.

Also, it's not a bad idea to read about specific interview questions and think about possible answers. There are lots of interview question books and information on the Internet. To find information online, try using Google or another search engine to search for the phrase "interview answers."

2.

Anticipate Questions

What to Think

You can anticipate the general questions that you will be asked.

What to Do

Think about the interview from the interviewer's point of view. Ask yourself, "If I were hiring someone for this position, what would I want to know?" After you develop some possible questions, write out your answers.

Also, don't forget to anticipate classic stock questions, such as the following:

- "Tell me about yourself."

- "Why are you interested in this job?"

- "What are your greatest strengths/weaknesses?"

To effectively answer these questions, develop and practice aloud answers that are based on your potential value to the company and that are unique to you and your personality.

3.

Prepare Success Stories

What to Think

The best predictor of how you will perform on a job is how you performed on prior jobs.

What to Do

Prepare six to eight success stories about things you did well at prior jobs. You can also use examples from prior situations with friends, family, organizations, or school.

A success story should include a brief description of the situation, the challenges you faced, what you did to overcome the challenges and, of course, the outcome. Each story should highlight one of your strengths, such as creativity, initiative, or good common sense. Success stories can be big accomplishments, such as saving the company a substantial amount of money, or small ones, such as helping to satisfy a customer.

Look for any openings in the interview to tell a success story. Even if you aren't asked a specific question, find ways of weaving them into the conversation.

4.

Know Your Strengths

What to Think

Knowing your strengths, talents, skills, values, and weaknesses will make you a more powerful and focused applicant.

What to Do

As part of your job-search process, make lists of the strengths, talents, skills, values, and weaknesses. Once you are aware of your characteristics, you can speak confidently about what you can contribute to an organization and can avoid talking about your weaknesses.

To make your strengths, talents, skills, and values seem more tangible—both to yourself and to others—tie them to specific situations where you demonstrated them. Also, include them in your success stories.

5.

Know the Company

What to Think

Many interviewers' biggest complaint is that applicants are not prepared for the interview. This communicates a lack of interest in the position. The more information you have about the company, the better prepared you will be to answer questions. In turn, you will communicate a greater interest and motivation in the position.

What to Do

Prepare, prepare, prepare. Regardless of the level of the job, it helps to know about the company, its markets, its strengths, and its challenges. It also helps to prepare pertinent questions based on your knowledge of the company.

With only modest preparation, you may actually end up knowing more about the company than the interviewer. This will help you sound knowledgeable and, in turn, interested in the position.

6.

Prepare Questions to Ask

What to Think

Interviewers like to be asked job- and company-focused questions. Your specific questions reveal that you have prepared for the interview and are interested in the position.

What to Do

Prepare a list of questions ahead of time and take the questions with you to the interview. When asked if you have any questions, take time to review your list and ask any questions that have not been answered during the course of the interview. It is perfectly okay to look at your list of questions; you do not have to have the list memorized.

7.

Prepare a List of Reminders

What to Think

When under stress in an interview, it is hard to remember all the questions you want to ask, all the examples of successes you want to talk about, and all the things you want to avoid.

What to Do

On the pad in your portfolio, write down the things you want to remember during the interview, such as your list of questions, the interviewer's name, as well as reminders to do such things as smile, relax, and avoid biting your nails.

Keeping other reference material handy is also a good idea. If you sent a cover letter that ties your qualifications to the job, bring it along. The same goes for the job posting, if you're responding to an ad or online job description.

8.

Keep Your Interview Skills Fresh

What to Think

Interviewing well is a critical job skill that, although used somewhat infrequently, has an enormous impact on careers.

What to Do

Develop interviewing skills like any other job skill. Stay current with the new developments in the field, such as behavioral questions and brain teasers that evaluate reasoning skills. The fact that you have not interviewed recently is no excuse for letting this critical skill become outdated.

9.
Don't Be Modest

What to Think

An interview is a time to brag about yourself and all the great things you can contribute to the company.

What to Do

Forget what you were told about not bragging. This is your time to shine. Before the interview, make a list of your skills and review the list. Bring the list with you and use it when it's time to tell the interviewer your strengths, your experiences, and what you can do for the company.

If you have ideas the company could use, share them. If you see new opportunities to bring in business, say so. If you can bring new methods, technologies, or specialized training or skills to their basic business challenges, let them know.

Don't leave a first, second, or third interview with the regret that "I should have mentioned my specialized training in X" or "I should have told them about the exact same problem I solved three years ago." Prepare to brag about yourself and share what you can do for them.

10.

Focus on the Process, Not the Outcome

What to Think

The actual outcome of the interview is beyond your control.

What to Do

Focus on the process of preparing and participating in the interview. Do not be tied to the outcome. As long as you are prepared and you manage the process well, you are doing all you can to get the job. If you managed the interview well and did not get the job, focus on the fact that you had a good interview and move on.

11.

Control the Screening Calls

What to Think

Someone from the company may call you at an unexpected time to do a screening interview on the phone. Often, it seems they call when you have just stepped out of the shower or are heading out the door. Even if it is a convenient time, you may not be mentally prepared for the call. It is only a screening interview, but it is an important first step in the process, and you need to be prepared.

What to Do

Defer the call until later. Let the caller know this is not a good time and schedule a time to speak with him or her later. You will not lose the opportunity.

Before the scheduled time, prepare for the call. Take out your resumé, review the job description, review your research on the company, and think through answers to questions you can predict.

The beauty of a phone interview is that no one can see what's on your desk or on your computer screen. It's okay to use brief bulleted notes to remind you of key points to discuss.

12.

Treat Every Contact as an Interview

What to Think

Every time you speak with a hiring manager from a potential employer, you should consider it an interview.

What to Do

Even though you may not be answering specific questions, keep in mind the basics: be positive, be curious about the person, ask good questions, and talk about what you have to offer the organization.

13.

Manage Every Contact

What to Think

Each and every contact you have with the company can affect the selection process. Thus, the interview starts with the first contact with the company and ends, hopefully, with the offer letter.

What to Do

At every point of contact with the company, be positive, enthusiastic, and focused on communicating how you can provide value to the organization. This includes such contacts as setting up your interview schedule, writing follow-up letters, and calling to follow up on the progress of the selection process.

14.

Schedule the Interview in the Morning

What to Think

Most hiring managers prefer to interview candidates in the morning. Morning is when they and the candidates are fresh and well rested. It's before the day fills with fires to be put out.

What to Do

If given the choice, try to schedule your interviews in the morning.

15.

Know Where to Go

What to Think

Many people go to the wrong place for their interview. This is particularly true when traveling a long distance.

What to Do

Be sure about the location of your interview. Take all relevant contact numbers with you, including the Human Resources contact, hiring manager, main office number, and any cell numbers provided to you. Put them in your planner next to the appointment time. This may seem like a nitpicky detail, but showing up at the headquarters instead of at a satellite location could mean a lost opportunity.

16.

Carry the Right Things

What to Think

Image is very important in an interview. You may be aware of how you are dressed and how you are groomed, but what you carry is also important. Do not go to an interview empty handed or too loaded down with a briefcase.

What to Do

Bring a professional-looking portfolio. A portfolio looks like a notebook with a leather or leather-like cover. Inside is a pad of paper and a sleeve for holding papers. Use the paper to take notes and the sleeves to carry copies of your resumé, recommendations, cover letter, and, if you have it, the job description. Do not bring a big cup of coffee or a can of soda. Only have a drink if offered by the interviewer.

17.

Bring Copies of Your Resumé

What to Think

Companies, even large sophisticated ones, are often not well organized when it comes to managing the interview process.

What to Do

Bring copies of your resumé and any other documentation you may have sent ahead. Bring one copy for each person with whom you are scheduled to interview. Even if the interviewer has a copy of your resumé, do not assume he or she has read it. Be prepared to point our relevant parts of your resumé, including jobs and experiences that make you a good candidate for the job.

18.

Prepare Your References

What to Think

Many companies ask for references, and contact them to ask about the applicant. References are typically called at the end of the selection process to see if any red flags are raised. Candidates give names of people they believe will give them positive references. Typically, people used as references are not well prepared to give a strong, job-specific reference.

What to Do

Coach your references. Give them a copy of your resumé. Let them know when they may be contacted by a company to which you are applying. Keep your references up to date about the jobs for which you are applying and inform them of any specific issues you'd like them to mention or avoid. Ask your references to contact you after they receive a call from one of your job leads.

19.

Present Yourself Well

What to Think

An interview is a very subjective process. Interviewers often select applicants based simply on which applicants they felt good about—or at least didn't feel uncomfortable about. It is important not to give an interviewer any reason to feel uncomfortable about you.

What to Do

Before your interview, do a last "bathroom" check. Make sure your buttons are buttoned, your collar is down, your tie is knotted tight, all your zippers are up, etc. Also, a breath mint may not be a bad idea.

20.
Be on Time

What to Think

Getting to an interview on time is one of those things we all know we should do, but sometimes life trips us up.

What to Do

Plan to arrive 15 minutes early. Then, plan on 15 minutes of extra time in traffic. In other words, plan to arrive in the parking lot 30 minutes before your scheduled interview time. Drive the route or practice getting to the location before the day of your interview. Know how to get there and how long it will take.

Once you've parked, spend any extra time reviewing your materials, research, and company information. Plan to walk in the door 15 minutes before your scheduled appointment time to complete any initial paperwork and to get a feel for the place. Browse the coffee tables in the reception area for company information, industry journals, or other "on-site intelligence."

21.
Allow Enough Time

What to Think

Interviews, especially ones that are going well, often take longer than the one hour allotted for the typical interview.

What to Do

Allow at least two hours for the interview. Some employers want to spend the best part of a day with you, have you meet a number of people, have you tour the facility, or give you pre-employment screening tests. Arrange your schedule so you do not feel rushed or inadvertently leave the impression you have more important things to do than participate in the interview.

22.
Be Friendly

What to Think

Each person you meet at the company, from the security guard at the front door to the department receptionist, may have a say about whether you're hired.

What to Do

Be friendly to everyone from the parking lot on in. Treat each person like a hiring manager. Be positive, friendly, and upbeat. Shake hands with people, look them in the eyes, and smile.

23.
Leave Off the Perfume

What to Think

Many people have chemical sensitivities. It is not a good idea to wear perfume or cologne to work or to an interview.

What to Do

Depend on a good shower to smell good. Do not wear perfume or cologne to the interview.

2

Interview Attitude: Being Prepared Mentally to Present Your Best

24.

Know They Are Interested

What to Think

You may be invited for an interview even if you don't seem to meet the job requirements.

What to Do

First, don't assume the company is making a mistake. Consider that the company finds you impressive in some unknown way. If the hiring manager didn't think you were qualified, he or she wouldn't waste time on an interview with you. Use the initial part of the interview to ferret out what led them to ask you to interview. You may be surprised to find that they are looking for something you were not aware you had.

25.

Remember You Are in an Interview

What to Think

The interview is a professional meeting to talk business. It is not about making a new friend.

What to Do

It is important to use professional language during the interview. Be aware of any inappropriate slang words or references to age, race, religion, politics, or sexual orientation. A misstep when talking about these topics could quickly doom your chances.

It is important to bring energy and enthusiasm to the interview and to ask questions, but do not overstep your boundaries by being overly friendly, chatty, or informal.

26.
Don't Be Offbeat

What to Think

A more dignified demeanor is back in style. Corporate dress styles have reverted to more business than business casual.

What to Do

Being offbeat or whimsical will not score you points. Remove the funny voicemail message from your answering machine, provide a good standard resumé without frills, and change your e-mail address to something professional sounding. Also, forget about sending balloons instead of a solidly written thank-you letter to follow up on your interview.

27.
Control Your Anxiety

What to Think

Interviews are very scary events, and most people tend to be anxious about them. You, however, are the one in control of how nervous you will be for the interview. Because you are in control, you can reduce your anxiety level.

What to Do

Be aware of what you are telling yourself. If you are thinking negative thoughts, such as, "I am not well qualified for the job" or "I am not prepared for the interview," you will feel anxious. Focus on positive thoughts, such as, "They wouldn't ask me to interview if they didn't think I was qualified. So, I must be qualified," or, "I could do an excellent job for this company." Your anxiety may not disappear, but it will be reduced, and will be easier to manage.

28.

Project Confidence

What to Think

You don't have to feel confident to look confident.

What to Do

Act confident, and you will appear confident. A firm hand-shake, good eye contact, and leaning forward in your chair will make you appear confident. Of course, it is best to actually *feel* confident. But if you are not feeling it, you can still appear confident to an outside observer. Concentrate on confident behaviors; the feelings will follow.

29.
Be Likeable

What to Think

Companies prefer not only experienced candidates, but also people who are a good fit. These are people who can work in teams, communicate effectively, be sensitive to social and cultural issues, and relate well to others. In other words, they are likeable.

What to Do

Be personable. Show your personality. Smile. Communicate with enthusiasm. Make small talk. Relate and bond. To do this effectively, you should be as relaxed as possible. Remember, interviews are gateways to opportunity, so be excited and upbeat.

30.

Be Positive—Always

What to Think

Companies and hiring managers are only interested in hiring positive people. If they hear any negativity, particularly about your last employer or boss, they will be hesitant to hire you. No one wants to work around negative people. After all, if you bad-mouth your previous employer, what's to stop you from saying negative things about the hiring manager to your next employer?

What to Do

Be totally positive about everything from the moment you enter the door. Be positive about your commute to the interview, be positive about your last job, and be positive about your last boss. Just be positive.

31.

Project a Positive Attitude

What to Think

Companies are starting to hire for attitude. The idea is that they can't transform even the most knowledgeable person into a good employee if they have the wrong temperament.

What to Do

Focus on communicating your attitude of self-motivation and commitment, and your goal of building good working relationships. Do not focus only on your skills and specific knowledge of the job. Present yourself as someone who will be a good employee, someone other people in the office will like, and someone about whom the hiring manager will not have to worry.

32.
Don't Try to Fit Perfectly

What to Think

There is rarely a time when a company finds an applicant who is absolutely perfect for the job. Each applicant has a mixture of strengths and weaknesses, and the company will select the applicant with the best fit.

What to Do

You don't need to approach the interview thinking that you have to present yourself as someone who is a perfect match for the job. When asked about your background and skills, talk honestly about your experiences. As the interview progresses, talk about the areas where you are a terrific fit for the job, as well as other areas where you would have to quickly attain new skills or knowledge. Your interviewer will appreciate that you're not trying to misrepresent yourself and are realistic about your fit with the position. This will be a mark in your favor.

33.
Sell Yourself

What to Think

Interviews are basically a sales situation. The buyer (hiring manager) is motivated to buy (hire) and is looking for the best product (applicant) that meets his or her needs. Buyers will shop around (interview), compare products (applicants), and make a buying decision (hire).

What to Do

Think like a salesperson. Ask good questions to understand what the company is looking for in an employee, and then link your features and benefits (skills and knowledge) to their needs. At the end of the sales pitch (interview), like any good salesperson, ask for the sale (position).

34.
Be a Solution to the Problem

What to Think

Consider a hiring situation like this: The hiring manager has a problem and the person being hired needs to fix it. The problem may be as simple as being shorthanded or as complicated as a declining stock price.

What to Do

First, either in the interview or through your research, determine the problem. Then present yourself in terms of how you can solve it.

35.
Be a Peer

What to Think

In an interview, the interviewer has the power to grant or deny you a job. Feeling less powerful undermines your confidence and self-esteem. The challenge is to restore the power balance.

What to Do

Think of the interview as a peer-to-peer conversation, in which two adults are discussing the position. Although you may be eager for the job, you still need to use your objective judgment to determine whether this job is a good fit for you. Engage in the conversation, ask questions, offer ideas, represent yourself, and ask for clarification of vague questions. Being in a peer conversation restores the balance.

36.

Focus on the Future

What to Think

Employers are interested in the future; resumés are the past. There is a tendency for applicants to lean too heavily on the resumé and talk about what they have done in the past. A good, solid resumé gets you the interview. Then the focus is on what you can do for the company moving forward.

What to Do

Focus on your performance on the prospective job. Project into the future exactly how you will perform the responsibilities of the job and how you will contribute to the company. Remember, stay future-focused. You should refer to your resumé only to support your ability to be a good performer in the position for which you are applying.

3

Interview Tactics: Making the Most of the Interview

37.

Answer the Three Key Questions

What to Think

An interview is designed to answer only three questions:

- Based on the candidate's background, experience, skills, and education, can he or she perform the tasks of this job and perform them well?

- Is the candidate interested in and motivated for this position?

- Will the candidate fit in the culture of the company? That is, will the candidate get along with his or her supervisor and the other employees, and will he or she take supervision?

Once these three questions are answered, other questions emerge such as those regarding compensation, relocation, travel, etc. The questions listed here must be answered satisfactorily before any other issues are considered, however.

What to Do

Focus your preparation on answering these three questions. You answer the first question by knowing the critical job requirements and understanding how your background, experience, skills, and education match those requirements. You answer the second question by preparing very well for the interview and showing energy and enthusiasm. The third question is addressed by how well you connect with the interviewer, as well as by you talking about traits and personality factors that make you a good employee.

38.
Make the First 10 Seconds Count

What to Think

Humans tend to form lasting impressions within the first 10 seconds of meeting someone. Chemistry, or lack thereof, is determined quickly. People form an opinion of someone based on appearance and body language.

What to Do

Make the first 10 seconds count. Demonstrate confidence. Stand straight, make eye contact, smile, and connect with a good, firm handshake. Practice these four things as part of your interview preparation.

39.

Initially, Focus on the Job

What to Think

The more you know about the company, the job, and the interviewer, the better you can relate your abilities to the position.

What to Do

At the beginning of the interview, encourage the interviewer to talk about the position, the company, and himself or herself. The longer the interviewer talks, the more information you'll have. At the same time, you'll have built greater trust with the interviewer. Trust is built when the interviewer is talking, not when *you* are talking.

If the interviewer starts by asking you questions, gently suggest that you can answer the questions better if you know more about the position first. Then draw out details. Get the interviewer talking with your list of prepared questions.

40.

Make the Interview a Conversation

What to Think

Typically, interviews are like interrogations, with the interviewer asking questions and the interviewee giving answers that he or she hopes are acceptable to the interviewer. No one likes to be interrogated. Being interrogated is stressful! People prefer to be in a conversation rather than an interrogation.

What to Do

Think of an interview as a conversation between two adults. During this conversation, information will be exchanged about a job opportunity, and both adults will decide whether the opportunity is a good fit. Because it is a conversation, both adults can ask questions, make comments, and talk about the interview situation itself. Being in a conversation, you can be more your authentic self.

41.

Listen, Then Respond

What to Think

When you are nervous about answering questions, you may tend to think about your answer before you hear the entire question.

What to Do

Be patient, listen to the entire question, and be sure you understand the question before answering. You can make sure you understand the question by asking more about what the interviewer wants to know. You can say, "I am not sure I understand your question. Can you tell me more about what you are asking?" No matter what, don't interrupt the interviewer before he or she is finished asking a question.

42.

Keep Answers Brief

What to Think

In a stressful situation, you may tend to ramble when answering a question.

What to Do

Keep answers brief and focused. Answers should be long enough to address the question but not so long as to contain unimportant information. To find out whether an answer was complete, ask the interviewer whether your response was on target and whether it contained enough information. For example, you might ask, "Did I answer your question, or is there more you would like to know?"

43.

Focus on the Positive

What to Think

In stressful situations, you may tend to focus on the negative or talk about negative experiences.

What to Do

Go into the interview thinking of what you have achieved and what you have to offer. Think of the ways you will benefit this company. Think of yourself as a valuable employee. Focus on the thought that the company would be lucky to have you. Also, remember the basic rule to always be positive about everything.

44.

Talk About Your Strengths

What to Think

A company is only interested your abilities, qualities, strengths, and experiences that apply directly to the job being filled.

What to Do

Identify your key strengths related to the position and be able to cite examples of these strengths through success stories.

Don't talk about strengths that don't apply to the job. This may only confuse the interviewer. He or she many think you do not understand the requirements of the job. For example, don't talk about your skill as a cook if you are interviewing to become a language-arts teacher. Remember the old sales axiom, "If they ask about X, 23d, and kangaroos, don't talk about Y, 47, and buffaloes."

Tailor and focus your message.

45.
Fit Yourself to the Job

What to Think

The interviewer is looking for candidates who are a good fit not just for the job description, but for the corporate culture. Interviewers don't come right out and ask, "Do you think you're a good fit for us?" The whole interview answers that question for them.

What to Do

Keep in mind that everything you do and say in an interview is being observed and judged to see how well you will fit in. Be as relaxed as you can—as much yourself as you can—but avoid saying or doing offbeat things that may be questionable within that culture.

If you can find out about the culture prior to the interview by talking to a current or former employee, you will have a better feel for what is acceptable behavior. Try to find out if the culture is loose and open or more structured and conservative. Then adjust accordingly within the range of what is comfortable for you.

46.

Communicate a Willingness to Learn

What to Think

Skills that are important today may not be in five years or even five months. Employers are interested in people who can learn new skills and will stay current with information, trends, and technologies.

What to Do

Talk about situations where you have mastered new skills and information. In addition, indicate an interest in learning new things. Talk about how you like to learn by doing such things as taking courses, self-study, or reading industry magazines.

If you do not have all the skills or knowledge for the position for which you are applying, be prepared to say how you will learn the skills and knowledge. Alternatively, point to similar situations in your past where you've successfully come up to speed on new information quickly. If this is a first job, you can refer to your school experience and cite an example of learning something challenging in school.

In some fields, such as technology, the ability to learn new things is almost more important than the knowledge you bring with you into a new environment.

47.

Be a Team Player

What to Think

These days, it is not enough just to be technically proficient. Companies are looking for team players who can communicate and who are politically aware.

What to Do

Be sure to talk about how well you get along with others or how well you function on teams. Be aware that working for a company requires you to act politically correct in the group environment. As always, it is best to include stories of when you actually did these things.

48.
Talk About Values and Work Style

What to Think

Today's ideal workers aren't who they used to be. These days, companies are looking for skilled and knowledgeable employees who take responsibility, monitor their own work, take initiative, and have values that are in alignment with the company's values.

What to Do

In addition to your skills and experience, be sure to communicate your values and work style. Try not to misrepresent these in order to impress the interviewer; just communicate your values and work style clearly. It is best to find out about any conflicts in the interview, and not on your first evaluation.

For example, if you are a creative person who likes change and innovation, it is probably best not to work in an overly structured, slow-moving organization. You will become quickly bored and frustrated with doing the routine tasks required for the business to be successful. On the other hand, if you like structure and do not enjoy change, maybe the job is for you.

49.

Communicate Conscientiousness and Stability

What to Think

Research studies have associated job performance with conscientiousness and emotional stability. Conscientiousness is reflected by how much the person cares about producing a quality product or service. Emotional stability is reflected by how much calmness and predictability a person has toward coworkers, customers, and problems in general.

What to Do

Find opportunities to introduce that you have these two qualities. Talk about your commitment to quality and your ability to get along with others. Relate an incident where you displayed these qualities. Remember, if you are interviewing at a company in which you do not care about the product or service it produces, it will be difficult to be successful there.

50.

Present Yourself as Flexible

What to Think

Organizations are all about change, adaptability, and flexibility, and they are looking for individuals who exhibit these qualities.

What to Do

Be prepared to talk about situations where you displayed flexibility, adaptability to new systems and processes, and a general comfort with change. Even if you are not asked specific questions about these qualities, look for opportunities to speak about them in the interview. Also, you can talk about using these qualities in non-job situations.

51.
Play It Conservative

What to Think

Most managers are nervous about making a bad hire. Even though they may talk about wanting creative, innovative individuals, they typically look for conservative, traditional, and safe people to hire.

What to Do

Try to come off as more traditional and conservative. You may be creative and innovative, and you certainly want to talk about those qualities, but present yourself on the traditional side. Wait until you get the job to display your inventive, imaginative, and quirky nature.

52.
Talk About Your Good Work Habits

What to Think

In addition to specific job skills, every hiring manager is looking for general traits of a good employee. These traits include punctuality, drive, reliability, honesty, self control, dedication, and efficiency.

What to Do

Find every opportunity in the interview to talk about situations that indicate you have these traits. Don't wait to be asked questions that elicit them. Talk about how you are always on time, how your attendance is consistent, how you work until the job is done, and how you pride yourself on your efficiency and effectiveness.

53.

Answer Questions Thoughtfully

What to Think

You will be asked questions that are difficult to answer and that require thought.

What to Do

Take your time answering questions. There is nothing wrong with asking for a moment to think about an answer. Answers that are carefully considered are typically better answers, and help you appear as a thoughtful, considered individual. It is important to give an answer to all questions even if it is an "I do not know." If you cannot answer an important question, you can support yourself by talking about how you would go about finding the answer. Remember, resourcefulness and initiative are key traits.

54.

Mention All Your Relevant Skills and Experiences

What to Think

An interviewer may not ask you questions about an important skill or experience. You are responsible for bringing out all the information about yourself that you think is important.

What to Do

If an interviewer has not asked a question about a certain skill or experience during the interview, bring it up in the context of, "There is something else you should know about me." Be sure to tie the skill or experience to how it will benefit the organization.

55.

Discussing Weaknesses

What to Think

We all have weaknesses, and it is common to be asked questions about your weaknesses.

What to Do

Remember that interviews are not places to discuss your weaknesses. You can avoid speaking about weaknesses by calmly stating that you are not aware of any weaknesses you have that would affect your performance on the job. You can add that if you were to discover a weakness on the job, you would address it, overcome it, or find a way to work with someone with complementary strengths. Again, be prepared to share a success story about how you dealt with a weakness on a prior job.

56.
Use Success Stories

What to Think

When interviewers ask for an example of a time when you did something, they are seeking a sample of your past behavior.

What to Do

Relate a specific example of a time when you exhibited a positive behavior. This is an opportunity to prove your ability and talk about your skills by relating a real-life event. Do not make an event up. A skilled interviewer will ask follow-up questions that are likely to trip you up. If you don't have a specific success story to tell, talk about what you would do in the situation or draw parallels to one of your success stories that reference similar traits and strengths.

57.

Admit When You Lack Experience

What to Think

There will be parts of the job for which you are well qualified and other parts of the job for which you may not have the specific background and experience the job requires.

What to Do

Remember, you do not have to be the perfect fit for the job, just the *best* fit. When answering questions about the parts of the job where you are strong, give longer answers. For questions that relate to your weaker areas, give briefer answers and refocus on the positive.

58.

Know How to Deal with Questions About Something You Haven't Experienced

What to Think

There may be a time in an interview when you are asked about something you have not done, thus you cannot relate a real-life story.

What to Do

State that you have not been involved in that specific situation. Then talk about what you would do if you were to be confronted with the situation. Say something like, "I have not had an experience with a manager I did not get along with, but if I did, I would handle it this way...."

59.

Communicate Non-Verbally

What to Think

Body language communicates volumes about you.

What to Do

Be sure to do the following in your interview:

- Make eye contact, but periodically break away. When you break away, do not look down; it has a connotation of submissiveness.

- Lean forward during a job interview. Leaning back conveys an attitude of being too relaxed.

- Don't show too much expression during interviews. You want to show some positive emotion, but it has to be understated and conservative.

- Feel free to laugh along with the interviewer, but don't erupt into laughter on your own. If you tend to have nervous laughter, stay aware of your nervousness and control your laughter.

60.
Answer the Tough Questions

What to Think

You will get a question that stumps you.

What to Do

Provide an answer to each question as best you can. If you get a tough question, take some time to formulate an answer either by paraphrasing the question, asking for clarification, or saying "That's a great question. I need a moment to think about that." Taking time to answer will show you are thoughtful and prudent.

You can find hundreds of generic questions online or in books. Select some of those questions and tailor your answers to your specific personality, speaking style, and situation. When looking at the questions, concentrate on the ones that are hard for you to answer. You will be fine with the easy questions in the interview, and the hard ones shouldn't be a problem if you're prepared.

61.
Ask Questions

What to Think

Asking questions demonstrates an interest in what goes on in the company and gives you the opportunity to find out if this is the right place for you.

What to Do

The questions you ask should be a combination of questions that you prepared prior to the interview and questions that come from listening to what the interviewer says during the interview.

The best questions are open-ended questions. For example, if, during the interview, you learn that the company is considering opening several new offices, you should probe further into this by asking the following:

- Could you tell me more about that?
- Could you be more specific about that?
- How long have you been planning this?
- What are your goals for the new offices?
- How will that affect someone new in this position?

62.
Listen Carefully

What to Think

From the very beginning of the interview, your interviewer will give you information, either directly or indirectly. If you don't pay attention, you will miss clues about what to focus on in the interview.

What to Do

Pay attention right away. Observe what is done and what is said. Listen and let the person know you heard what was said.

Remember, during the first part of an interview, the interviewer talks while you listen. Do not mentally prepare your answers while the interviewer is speaking; just listen. After you have heard about what the job requires and what the hiring manager wants and needs, spend your time bridging your skills and experiences to these wants and needs.

63.
Ask for Feedback

What to Think

You should know how the interview went from the interviewer's perspective and whether you are being considered as a candidate for the position.

What to Do

At the end of the interview, ask for feedback. Say something such as, "Based on what you have learned about me from the interview, what do you think about my candidacy for this position?" Or ask a more direct question, such as, "So, do I get the job?" Sometimes, this direct approach, if delivered with good humor, may yield surprising results—like the answer, "Yes!" Typically, however, you will get a non-committal answer such as, "We have other candidates to interview." Even if you receive a negative response, it is far better to know immediately than to wait for a rejection letter or, worse, no contact at all.

64.

Link Your Goals to the Company's Goals

What to Think

Hiring managers generally dislike interviewing, hiring, and training new people. Staff turnover is a costly and stressful issue for organizations, so most hiring managers will want to hire a person who can find a place in the organization and stay put. Therefore, the hiring manager may ask you about your five-year goals.

What to Do

Communicate that you are a team player who will help the company over the long term. You can do this by expressing goals that can be met within the organization over the next several years. Tie your growth and goals to things you can accomplish within the organization. These goals should be of value to the organization, not just to you personally.

65.
Repeat Yourself for Emphasis

What to Think

Interviewers may interview multiple candidates or may not be good listeners. Thus, they may miss your primary strengths.

What to Do

Don't be concerned about being repetitious. Decide on your five main strengths and bring them up numerous times during the interview.

One way to know what to repeat is to ask yourself the question, "After the interview, what do I want the interviewer to think about me?" For example, if you want to communicate that you are efficient, talk about your efficiency and relate a situation in which you applied your efficiency. You can also talk about bringing efficiency to the job. Or you could mention how you strive for a balance between efficiency and effectiveness, and focus on doing the right things and doing things right.

66.
Display Knowledge of the Job

What to Think

It is important for the interviewer to know you are knowledgeable about the industry or position for which you are applying. Depending on the level of the job, this might include being aware of industry-wide trends or knowing what is the hardest part of doing a particular job.

What to Do

Use words specific to that industry or job. Research the company, read the job description, and talk with people who work in the field or in the job. Then, based on this information, memorize five to 10 jargon words from the industry. Finally, use those words during the interview. For example, if you are applying to work maintenance for an airline, know that "turnaround time" for preparing an airplane is important. If you are applying for a position as a project manager, know that "risk management" and "risk mitigation" are critical functions.

67.
Be Specific

What to Think

All candidates present themselves in the best possible light. They talk about their best qualities and claim to be terrific employees. Your claims will be the same, thus it is difficult for the interviewer to tell the difference between candidates.

What to Do

Include as much concrete, quantifiable data as possible. Interviewees tend to talk in generalities, and generalities fail to convince interviewers that the applicant has the required skills and attitudes. Include measurable information and provide details about specific accomplishments when discussing your strengths. These can be on-the-job or off-the-job experiences.

68.
Put Yourself on the Team

What to Think

Your challenge is to convince the interviewer that you will perform well on the job. To achieve this, it is helpful for the interviewer to see you in the position as an insider.

What to Do

Put yourself on the employer's team. Show you are thinking like a team member by using the employer's name and mentioning the organization's products or services. For example, you might say "As an employee at (employer's name), I would carefully consider the best uses of (product name) to increase its sales." Some applicants have even taken this one step further and brought writing samples, mock reports, or "white papers" they've written that incorporate the company's logos, tagline, or brands. This can be a powerfully suggestive move that puts you on the inside track as someone "who practically works here already!"

69.

Focus on What You Can Bring

What to Think

The ultimate goal of an interview is to communicate clearly what value you will bring to the company. The interview is about what you will do for the company, not what the company will do for you.

What to Do

All statements should be focused on what you can contribute to the company. Statements such as, "This is a good career opportunity for me," "Working here will cut my commute in half," or "I haven't worked on this type of product before and it will give me good experience," is not focusing on the company. Keep in mind that it is all about what you can contribute to them.

70.

Talk About Responsibilities and Accomplishments

What to Think

Hiring managers are interested in what you will bring to the position.

What to Do

You can best communicate what you have to offer by talking about what you have done at previous jobs. Practice describing your prior experience in terms of your responsibilities and accomplishments at each prior job. Then, in the interview, talk about responsibilities and accomplishments as more than titles and positions. Remember, you should relate what you have done in the past to what you will do in the future for this company.

71.

Take Notes

What to Think

Interviews are inherently stressful situations. Even if you follow all the suggestions in this book, you may still feel nervous in the interview. Under stress, people tend to forget things.

What to Do

Take notes in the interview. Taking notes gives the interviewer the impression that the applicant is taking the interview seriously and that he or she is organized. In addition, you can refer to your notes when you write your follow-up letter.

72.
Take the Tests

What to Think

Companies are desperate to hire qualified applicants who will fit their culture. Because the hiring process is subjective and inefficient, companies are increasingly turning to objective personality tests and, depending on the position, tests for skills such as writing, grammar, and software proficiency.

What to Do

If you want to be considered for the job, go along with the testing. If you know beforehand that there will be skills tests, try to brush up on your writing, grammar, and software skills. Don't worry about the personality tests; you cannot outguess them. You have to trust that the company has selected tests that predict who will do well on the job. Keep in mind that even if you are feeling desperate, you do not want a job in which you will not succeed. Hopefully, the tests will make the hiring decision more accurate.

73.

Talk About Skills in Demand on All Jobs

What to Think

Employers look for new sets of skills in addition to basic knowledge. The skills most in demand are as follows:

- Clear communication in print and in person
- Self-motivation
- Time management
- Relationship building
- Salesmanship
- Problem-solving
- Information evaluation
- Leadership
- Application of technology
- Creative thinking

What to Do

Find every opportunity to speak about these skills, even if you are not asked about them directly. Bring up situations where you displayed these skills, talk about the importance of the skills, and talk about how you will build and maintain these skills. Simply recognizing these are important skills and speaking about them will strengthen your interview. To remind yourself to talk about these skills, include them on your written reminder list of things to talk about in the interview.

74.

Get Contact Information

What to Think

It is important to have the correct contact information for the interviewer so you can follow up.

What to Do

You should request a business card and ask if you can contact the interviewer with any additional questions and to follow up. Be sure to get contact information from each person with whom you interview.

75.

Close Strong

What to Think

The interview will come to an end and you should be prepared to provide a strong closing.

What to Do

Wrap up your interview by offering the interviewer a short, concise summary of your qualifications and stress your interest in the position. Basically, ask for the job. Thank the interviewer for taking the time to meet with you. Then, keep the process going by asking what the next step is in the interviewing process, how long you should wait before following up, and the best way for you to follow up.

76.

Be Tactful if You Don't Want the Job

What to Think

You will find that not every job is right for you, and that you may turn down jobs offered to you. You may be well aware during the interview that you would not accept the job, even if it were offered.

What to Do

It is appropriate to let the interviewer know during the interview that you are not a good match for the position, or that you do not think you could provide the success factors that the job requires. Don't burn bridges, however. Be sure to end the interview with tact and sensitivity.

Remember, just as you would feel rejected if you were not offered the job, the interviewer may feel rejected by you not pursuing the job. When turning down the job, state your decision in terms of not being able to do the best job for the company. This is actually a true statement. If you don't like the job, the company, or the boss, or if it does not pay enough, you are not a good fit for the position.

4

Managing the Interviewer: Connect Through Curiosity and Conversation

77.

Connect with the Interviewer

What to Think

No matter how good your resumé looks, how good you look, how well you answer questions, or how well you can do the job, you will not get the job unless you make a personal connection with the interviewer.

What to Do

When the introductions are being made at the start of the interview, look directly into the interviewer's eyes and give that person your warmest smile. Then show your interest in making a genuine connection with the interviewer by being curious about him or her. At some point in the interview, ask the interviewer how he or she got to his or her current job. This question focuses on the interviewer, allowing that person to talk about himself or herself. After all, that is everyone's favorite topic!

78.

Be Interested in the Interviewer

What to Think

Interviewers are people, too. They like to talk about themselves and have others show interest in them.

What to Do

Being curious about other people is part of being likeable and getting along well with others. Be genuinely interested in your interviewers. Ask about them, their experience in the company, and their path to their current position. Be engaged about what they are saying. If they ask a question about how you would handle a certain situation, answer the question first. Then ask them how *they* would handle the situation or if they've experienced something similar.

79.
Find Commonalities

What to Think

People tend to like people with whom they have something in common, whether it's an alma mater, a past employer, a former colleague, the same hometown, or the love of a sports team.

What to Do

Try to find a point in common and talk about it. Look around the office for clues or ask a question about how the interviewer got to the position he or she is in. Look and listen for ways in which you are similar to the interviewer. Once you have discovered a similarity, bring it up in light conversation. Light conversation is a good way to get to know the interviewer on a more personal level, and to let the interviewer know you more personally.

80.
Adjust to the Interviewer

What to Think

People tend to be attracted to people who are like them.

What to Do

Observe your interviewer and match his or her style and pace. If he or she tends to be more formal, be more formal yourself. If he or she speaks slowly and deliberately, speak in the same way. If he or she is relaxed and joking, then you can risk some levity. However, never go beyond your comfort level in terms of being yourself.

81.

Focus on the Needs
of the Hiring Manager

What to Think

The hiring manager's bottom line is what you will contribute to his or her life at work. Even though the discussion focuses on the organization, the hiring manager is thinking, "How will this person improve my life?"

What to Do

Ask questions that elicit information about the hiring manager's personal needs within the organization and talk about how you will address those needs. Listen for the hiring manager's personal orientations and goals. Then weave into your discussion how you are uniquely qualified to meet those goals and that you share those same values and priorities.

82.

Establish Relationships with Everyone

What to Think

The hiring manager is often surrounded by people who have a role in the selection process, from input about the decision to arranging interview schedules.

What to Do

Establish relationships with everyone, particularly the person responsible for scheduling and managing the interview process. The scheduler is often more accessible than the hiring manager. If you have a good relationship with that person, he or she may share inside information with you.

83.

Give Genuine Compliments

What to Think

People like to feel good about themselves. To put an interviewer in a better mood, offer a compliment.

What to Do

Say a nice word or two about the company, the office's location, or the view from the window—something that will make the interviewer feel good. Paying a genuine compliment also indicates you are a positive person, an attitude hiring managers like in candidates.

Keep your compliment simple and safe. Avoid any compliments about personal appearance; they may come across as too intimate. Mention how friendly everyone is or compliment the company based on your research. Be sure the compliment is genuine. Giving inauthentic compliments will sound phony and hollow.

84.

Manage a Bad Interviewer

What to Think

About 90 percent of interviewers are not trained, which means you will likely have an unskilled interviewer. Unskilled interviewers can ask vague questions and leave you guessing about what they want to hear. Once you start guessing, you run the risk of giving off-focus answers that don't help your candidacy.

What to Do

When you are asked an unclear question, ask for clarification. Say something like, "Can you tell me more about what you mean?" Once you have answered the question, you can ask for feedback on your answer. "Did I answer your question or is there more information in which you are interested?" With a weak interviewer, answer questions like a good politician. Regardless of the question, weave in talking points and success stories that you've prepared ahead of time.

85.

Guide the Interview

What to Think

Many hiring managers are poor interviewers. They will not be skilled at finding out your features that will benefit their organization. You will find that many hiring managers talk a lot about the job and themselves rather than getting to know your strengths.

What to Do

If you walk out of the interview without having presented all your strengths and skills relative to the job, don't blame the interviewer. Be prepared to actively guide the interview. Whenever possible, take the opportunity to speak about what you can contribute. Also, it is always best to prepare an interview presentation to take with you to the interview so you have a written document you can use to guide the interview.

86.

Manage an Unstructured Interview

What to Think

An interviewer may have a non-directive interview style. This means the interview will be unstructured—more like a loose conversation than one with a lot of specific questions. The interviewer may do all the talking or very little.

What to Do

In this situation, you have to take control. Talk about how your skills fit the position and ask good job-related questions.

In a way, this can be an easier interview. You drive the conversation to the points *you* want to make, and can seek the information you need to make an informed decision about the position, company, culture, and other factors affecting your potential success.

87.

Manage the Stress Interview

What to Think

A *stress interview* is one in which the interviewer is aggressive, disagrees with the interviewee, and pushes the applicant for answers. The stress interview is designed to identify individuals who are unable to handle the stress they would encounter on the job.

What to Do

Realize that this is a stress interview. Don't take it personally. Smile inside, knowing that you are aware of what the interviewer is up to.

Under stress, people tend to speed up and lose their best judgment. Breathe! Also, take your time responding to the interviewer's questions. Remember, on the job, there is always a time to evaluate a situation before responding.

88.

Manage the Behavioral Interview

What to Think

Behavior-based questions in interviews are becoming more popular. The premise behind behavioral interviewing is that the most accurate predictor of future performance is past performance in similar situations. Behavior-based questions consist of asking about a situation in which you performed a particular behavior.

What to Do

Be prepared to answer detailed questions about a number of specific situations in which you performed well. These are your prepared "success stories." The more success stories you have, the better.

One story can be used to answer a number of behavioral questions. For example, your success story about solving a customer's problem can be used to address questions about critical thinking, taking initiative, willingness to learn, self-confidence, teamwork, and professionalism.

89.

Manage Illegal Questions

What to Think

During an interview, you may be asked questions not permissible by law. Typically, such questions focus on your marital status, parental responsibilities, age, weight, health, race, nationality, religious affiliations, or political affiliations. Legal questions are ones that relate to the position's requirements and your ability to meet those requirements.

What to Do

You have the right not to answer illegal questions. If you choose to answer these questions, first, ask how the question relates to the job responsibilities and then craft your answer accordingly. For example, questions about family may be a way of asking if you will be dedicated to the job. Respond to questions about your family or plans for a family by stating you are aware of the demands of the job and are committed to meeting those demands.

90.
Manage Brain-Teaser Questions

What to Think

There is an emerging trend, especially in technical fields, to ask brain-teaser questions. For example, you may be asked, "How many quarters, placed one on top of the other, would it take to reach the top of the Empire State Building?" Or, "How many tons does the Washington Monument weigh?"

What to Do

The goal of brain-teaser questions is to get an idea of an applicant's reasoning ability. Don't be concerned about getting the absolute right answer; focus on developing a logical approach to solving the problem. The more creative and well-reasoned your response, the better.

91.

Manage Questions About Existing Company Problems

What to Think

Interviewers may ask how you would solve a specific problem they are facing right now in their organization. This is a tricky question.

What to Do

Don't try to suggest specific or tactical solutions to existing problems. You don't have enough information, and you may suggest solutions that have already been tried or that are unworkable, which will just disappoint the interviewer. Instead, talk about a general approach or a strategic solution that you would use to solve that type of problem. If possible, relate the problem to a situation in a prior job and talk about the specifics of how you solved that problem. Mention the fact that without knowing further details, this may or may not be a workable solution to their current challenge.

92.

Manage the Compensation Question

What to Think

Compensation is one of the tricky areas in a job interview. If you speak about it too soon, you may seem too money-focused or you may limit your negotiating leverage. If you don't speak about it soon enough, you may be interviewing for a job you wouldn't take because it does not pay enough.

What to Do

Let them bring up the subject of money. If you are asked about your salary expectations early in the process, say you would rather postpone that discussion until you have more information about the position. Alternatively, try to get the interviewer to state a number by asking, "Could you tell me the salary range budgeted for the position?" Once you hear the range, you can decide whether the salary is adequate for your needs.

5

THE INTERVIEW PRESENTATION: BE MORE PERSUASIVE WITH A PRINTED PRESENTATION

93.
Present to Win

What to Think

An interview is basically a sales call. Having a well-developed targeted "sales" presentation will differentiate you and help you clearly communicate how you are a good candidate for the position.

What to Do

Develop a presentation that you print, bind, and bring with you to the interview. Bring a copy for each person with whom you will be interviewing. Once you have given your presentation, the bound document makes a great leave-behind.

94.

Appeal to Visual Learners with an Interview Presentation

What to Think

Interviews are generally verbal and auditory. The problem is, only 20 percent of the population is composed of auditory learners (that is, people who learn by listening). In contrast, 40 percent of the population are visual learners (people who learn by looking or reading). The better an interviewer learns and retains what you tell him or her, the better your ability to persuade the interviewer of your value.

What to Do

Develop an interview presentation to print, bind, and take with you to an interview. The presentation should clearly communicate how you match the critical requirements of the position. Use the presentation in the interview, and then leave it behind as a written reminder of your interview.

95.

Gain Value from Preparing a Presentation

What to Think

Just the process of thinking through and preparing an interview presentation will be very valuable. After you develop your presentation, you will feel more confident and prepared for your interview.

What to Do

Even if you decide not to use a printed presentation in your interview, develop one. Thinking through how your background, skills, and experience match the job requirements and the value you bring to a job will give you the insight to answer a lot of interview questions.

96.

Don't Worry About Being an Expert Presenter

What to Think

An interview presentation is not a "front of the room," stand-up presentation. Rather, it is a conversation starter and a conversation guide. So don't worry about your presentation skills.

What to Do

Use the presentation to begin and support a conversation. During the presentation, ask questions of the interviewer and respond to the interviewer's questions. Don't be strictly focused on getting through your presentation. Be focused on communicating with the interviewer and responding with the information in which the interviewer expresses interest.

97.
Listen as You Present

What to Think

An interview presentation is a combination of talking, asking questions, and listening. The percentage should almost be 50/50 talking and listening.

What to Do

Before the interview, do your research and prepare your presentation. While in the interview, use your presentation to provide a guideline for the content you want the hiring manager to know about. Of course, during the interview, you are sure to learn new information, which should be included in your talk. So use the presentation to introduce information but listen as well as talk.

98.

Use the Presentation as a Guide

What to Think

Some people get concerned that the interviewer will be annoyed if the candidate tries to control the interview. An interview presentation is an interview "guide," not a way to control the interview.

What to Do

Introduce your presentation by asking permission to present it. Be interactive during your presentation. Maintain eye contact with the interviewer(s) and carry on a conversation. Always follow the interviewer's direction. If he or she wants to pursue a certain line of questions or digress from the presentation, do not hesitate to go with the flow.

99.
Keep It Brief

What to Think

It is difficult—if not impossible—for people to read and listen at the same time. If the interviewer is busy reading your presentation, he or she will not be listening to you.

What to Do

Your presentation should consist of very brief bullet points. The writing should not communicate details; it should serve only as an introduction and a placeholder for your main points. As a rule of thumb, your text should not be more than two lines in length (or 140 characters, like a Twitter tweet).

Use your bullet points to introduce information you want the interviewer to know. Then talk about and engage the interviewer in conversation about the information. In this way, you get your information across while maintaining the interviewer's attention.

100.

Be Aware That Your Presentation Is Your Understanding, Not Fact

What to Think

Your presentation represents your understanding of the position prior to the interview. With some basic research about the company, position, and the industry, your presentation will be mostly accurate. However, there may be some gaps or misinterpretations about the job and the company. These gaps or misinterpretations are not a problem and will be clarified in the interview.

What to Do

Position your presentation as your current understanding, not something that is definitive. You can say, "My presentation is based on my research and understanding of the position at this point. I am sure I will learn additional information during our interview." Listen for things you may have missed or things that need to be changed, and weave them into your presentation.

101.

Ask for Permission to Present

What to Think

Some interviewers have a well-established format for the interview that does not accommodate an interview presentation. Other interviewers may just be uncomfortable with a new approach to interviewing.

What to Do

Introduce your presentation and then ask permission to present it. For example, you might say, "I have developed a presentation about my background and skills and how they match the critical requirements of this position, and why I am a good candidate for the job. May I share it with you?" Do not be concerned or thrown if the interviewer says no (although this happens very infrequently). Simply put your presentation aside and go on with the interview. Introduce the information you wrote into your presentation when you have the opportunity. Also, be sure to leave your presentation with the interviewer; it's an excellent leave-behind, which no interviewer refuses.

102.

Use Your Presentation to Communicate Interest and Motivation

What to Think

Interest and motivation for a job is one of the top two or three most important selection criteria. The more interested and motivated you are, the greater your likelihood of getting the job. Taking the time and effort to develop an interview presentation will automatically impress the interviewer with your interest and motivation for the job.

What to Do

Introduce you presentation by stating your interest and motivation. For example, you might say, "I am very interested and motivated for this position. Because of my interest, I have put together a presentation about how my background and skills match the critical requirements of this job and why I am an excellent candidate for this position. May I share it with you?"

103.
Present Your Benefits

What to Think

Items for sale have both features and benefits. A *feature* is a fact about the item, something it has or does. Features are easy to identify and understand. *Benefits* are what a buyer gets from purchasing the item. It answers the question, "What's in it for me?" Most job candidates only talk about their features—their skills sets, experience, education, etc. Hiring managers are most interested, however, in benefits—what value a candidate brings to the organization.

What to Do

Throughout your presentation, always link a feature to a benefit. For example, "I have six years of experience selling copiers in this market (feature). Therefore, I will be able to quickly establish a sales pipeline and reach sales goals four to six months faster than anyone else (a huge benefit)." Don't leave it up to the hiring manager to figure out your benefits. Lay them out clearly.

104.
Clarify the Job Requirements First

What to Think

You need to know what the job requires in order to convince the interviewer you can do the job and that you are the best candidate. Thus, a "needs" analysis is the first step in a job interview.

What to Do

In your interview presentation, first list six or seven critical requirements of the position as you understand them. You can introduce your list of critical requirements using the following statement: "I have written a list of the critical requirements of the position as I understand them. I would like to discuss the list with you so we have a mutual understanding of the requirements of the position."

Then, start your presentation by discussing the requirements with the interviewer. Once you and the interviewer have come to an understanding about the details of the requirements, you can clearly communicate how your skills and background match the requirements.

105.

Match Your Experience and Skills to the Job Requirements

What to Think

The most important criterion in the selection process is how well you can do the job. You must clearly communicate how your background and skills match the critical requirements of the job and will enable you to perform well.

What to Do

Take the job requirements—no more than seven—and list up to three jobs, experiences, or educational courses you've undertaken that prove you have the skills required to do the job. Speak to each point during your presentation, emphasizing how what you did in that situation is related to the critical requirements for this job. Use numbers and facts whenever possible.

106.

Differentiate Yourself with Additional Areas of Expertise

What to Think

If the hiring company has done a good job of screening applicants, all candidates will be capable of performing the basic
requirements of the job. Your task is to first reinforce the fact
that you can do the job, and then to differentiate yourself from
the rest of the pack. You can do this by presenting your additional areas of expertise that will provide extra value to the
position.

What to Do

Include a list of additional areas of expertise in your presentation. Introduce these areas by suggesting they could add a
great deal of value, indicating how they might add value, and
conveying your level of expertise. These "value adds" must
be related to the position but may not be in immediate
demand. For example, if you are interviewing for a journalist
position, an additional area of expertise might be Web development. Web development is not a requirement of the job,
but it may be very valuable if the organization wants to set up
a Web site for its articles. Another example of an additional
area of expertise might be the ability to speak a foreign language. How might speaking that language add value, and
what is your level of proficiency?

107.

Present Your Success Stories

What to Think

People love stories. Stories bring information and facts alive. Telling stories about times in your career when you were at your best will make you more memorable and persuasive.

What to Do

Include a list of story headlines in your presentation. Headlines should be brief, descriptive, and eye-catching—for example, "Implemented New Business Process, Achieving $50,000 in Savings in 6 Months." During your interview, tell a story about how you achieved this success. Include the situation, the obstacles you had to overcome, the details of what you did, and the outcome. Also include a list of skills you used, such as persuasion, listening, analysis, team work, etc.

108.
Add Value Quickly

What to Think

Everyone wants a return on their investment (hiring decision), and they want it fast. By showing how you will quickly add value to the company, you will differentiate yourself and instill confidence in the hiring manager that you are the best candidate.

What to Do

Develop a 30- and 60-day strategic action plan. Lay out your goals for the first 30 and 60 days. Make the goals specific, and talk about how you will achieve them.

As with the rest of your presentation, position the goals as being based on the job as you understood it while you were developing your presentation. Let the hiring manager know the goals are flexible and open to change as you get to know the job better.

109.

Fit the Culture

What to Think

Today, companies do not base hiring decisions just on skills and experience. Companies hire people they like and who fit in their culture. Likeability and culture fit are not easily communicated in an interview. As a result, the hiring decision becomes very subjective.

What to Do

Use your presentation to communicate your qualities and character traits that make you successful on the job. These qualities might include "active learner," "collaborative," or "able to step up to conflict." Be prepared to talk about these qualities, how they operate at work, examples of when you used them, and how they will benefit your new employer.

110.

Sum Up Your Best "Selling" Points

What to Think

Even with a written presentation, the interviewer will retain only a limited amount of the information, so repetition is powerful. Interview presentations have a lot of good, targeted, and persuasive information the interviewer should remember, however. It is helpful to choose the most persuasive points—somewhere between five and seven points should do—and state them again for reinforcement.

What to Do

Make a list of what you believe to be the most powerful reasons you are the best candidate for the position. Speak to each point, focusing on the benefits you will bring to the company. Do not worry that you have already mentioned these points. Repeating them will improve retention and persuasion.

111.

Include Good Questions

What to Think

At some point in every interview, the interviewer asks, "Do you have any questions for me?" Having good, insightful questions is very important. Plus, having written questions as part of your interview presentation will ensure they get answered.

What to Do

Include a list of questions in your presentation. Questions should reflect your knowledge of the industry, company, and position. Don't worry if your questions have already been answered during the interview. Just having them in writing shows an excellent level of preparation and interest.

112.
Ask for the Sale

What to Think

All good sales presentations ask for the sale. Your interview presentation should do the same. Be aware, however, that if you ask a direct question such as, "Will you hire me?" you will probably be put off by the classic dodge, "We really like you but we have more people to interview."

What to Do

In your list of printed questions, include the question "How and when would you like me to follow up with you?" This essentially asks for a second meeting or contact, which works well as a sales closing technique. Once the interviewer tells you how and when to contact him or her, you have that person's "permission" to be assertive and follow up.

6

AFTER THE INTERVIEW: IT'S NOT OVER YET

113.
Be Prepared to Wait

What to Think

The selection process takes longer than an applicant would like, and often longer than the employer predicted.

What to Do

At the end of the interview, ask about the selection process and when you can expect to hear back about the job. If the interviewer doesn't contact you as promised, don't be surprised—it happens a lot.

Waiting for that call is one of the most difficult parts of the interview process. It's sometimes difficult to resist the temptation to call too soon or too often. If a week goes by after the decision was supposed to have been made, call and ask if the position is still open. If the answer is yes, ask if you're still under consideration.

Do not be surprised, or take it personally, if you are not notified when you were not selected. Companies are notoriously bad about notifying rejected applicants.

114.

Remember the Selection Process Is Subjective

What to Think

Research shows that the typical employment interview is only 57 percent accurate as a predictor of future performance. That is not much better than flipping a coin.

What to Do

Lighten up on yourself and relax. Even if you are the best-qualified candidate, there is a chance that you will not be selected. On the flip side, if you *aren't* the best qualified, there is a chance that you *will* be selected. Go figure! All you can do is be prepared and do all the right things in the interview. Then it is up to the subjective judgment of the hiring manager.

115.

Know This Isn't Your Only Interview

What to Think

Interviews are high-pressure situations. When you have one, you will typically be very focused on how much you want the job. Being under pressure in a situation where you really want something very badly and being worried about not getting it is very stressful.

What to Do

Think about the fact that this is not the only interview you will have. You landed this interview, and you will land more. If you don't get this job, it might hurt your ego, but it does not mean you won't get the next job—which may actually be a better fit.

116.

Learn from Every Interview

What to Think

A job search typically consists of a number of interviews with different companies. Each interview provides experience and an opportunity to learn.

What to Do

Debrief after each interview, either with another person or with yourself. Think about what went well and what didn't. Reflect on the questions you asked, how well you listened, and how well you were able to link your skills and experiences to the interviewer's needs. Write down three things you did particularly well and three things upon which you would like to improve. Include the latter on the reminder list that you bring to your next interview.

117.

Maintain an Active Search

What to Think

Depending on your situation, you may be feeling frantic about landing a job. It is important not to appear or to act desperate with interviewers.

What to Do

Be engaged in an active job search with a lot of activity. Talk to a lot of people. Target 20 to 30 companies and explore a good range of options. Actively searching will reduce your feelings of desperation and will lessen the perceived importance of any single interview, which will make you more relaxed and more engaged in the interview. You cannot control whether you get the job; you can only control whether you have a good interview. Remember, you may be just one great interview away from your dream job!

118.

Determine the Job Fit Before Salary Talks

What to Think

The initial interview(s) determines your fit for the position and your desire for the job. There will be plenty of opportunity to talk about the nitty-gritty details of the job, like salary, vacation, holidays, and health care coverage later in the selection process.

What to Do

Don't ask about compensation details during the first interview. After you have sold yourself and are close to receiving a job offer, you can get those answers and negotiate the compensation.

119.

Always Negotiate Salary

What to Think

Rarely is a salary non-negotiable. The company has gone through a lot of time and effort to, find, interview, and select someone to hire. Once they've chosen someone, they don't want to settle for whoever was second best. They want *you*, and they are willing to negotiate to get you.

What to Do

Do not take the first salary offer. In a professional, non-aggressive way, simply express disappointment in the offer and ask if they can do better. Even a simple statement such as, "That's a bit less than I was hoping for. Can you do better?" can result in a higher salary. Be prepared to answer the question, "What were you hoping for?" The number you say should be bold but realistic.

120.

Negotiate Salary After an Offer

What to Think

The best time to negotiate a salary is after you have received a job offer—but before you accept the position. Once on the job, you will (hopefully) receive regular raises and bonuses, but these will be based on your starting salary.

What to Do

When salary becomes an issue, be prepared to discuss it based on knowledge. Research what people in comparable positions make in your geographic area. If the interviewer quotes a salary range that is low, you can quote the salary paid by other companies.

121.

Always Follow Up

What to Think

You should follow all interviews with a follow-up letter. This letter is an opportunity to support and possibly strengthen your candidacy for the position. Because there will typically be several top candidates for the position, this follow-up letter can help nudge the decision in your favor.

What to Do

Think of the follow-up letter as the continuation of your interview sales pitch. Use it to strengthen the interviewer's perception of you by reinforcing your strong points and addressing any concerns you believe the interviewer might have. This is also a great vehicle to add any related skills, abilities, or interests, and any other information that you did not mention during the interview. The note can be via e-mail or hard copy. To know which one to use, ask the interviewer, "How would you prefer me to follow up? By e-mail or by letter?"

122.

Follow Up with Everyone

What to Think

Each person you interview with will have a say about whether you get hired.

What to Do

Send follow-up letters to each person with whom you interviewed, preferably within 24 hours of the interview. Be brief, but personalize the letters to each individual. Thank each interviewer for his or her time, reiterate your strengths and your interest in the company, and communicate excitement about the position. This task will be much easier if you take notes during your interview. Also, be sure to get each interviewer's business card.

123.

Evaluate Whether the Job Is for You

What to Think

Even if you feel desperate for a job, remember that a bad job can be worse than no job at all. If you take a bad job, you may suffer and then lose the job. This will put you back where you are now—and add the challenge of explaining to the next hiring manager why you had your last job for only a brief duration.

What to Do

Use the interview to determine whether the job is for you. Listen carefully to what the hiring manager requires for success on the job. Ask good questions about the job and then think about your fit for the position, the company culture, and the manager. Remember, you are interviewing and qualifying your next employer just as much as the company is interviewing and qualifying its next employee!